The Skinny Little Book Of

Word Power

Words To Get You Going And Keep You Going

Nikki Nev McMillen

ISBN: 9798845926685

DEDICATION

To my mum, my sister, my daughter, and my extended family. Love you lots, and always remember…

"Hakuna Matata"

In loving memory of my dad.

CONTENTS

PREFACE

Hello fellow human, and welcome to this experience!

Because that's what it is; an experience. Every time you open a book, have a conversation with someone, or lose yourself in thought, you're engaging in an experience. And in this busy world, I think we can sometimes forget that. So, I invite you to slow down, become present, connect with these words, connect with yourself, and then afterwards go and connect with others about the fruits of your experience with this Skinny Little Book.

I have to start off by saying how incredibly excited and grateful I am to have published this book, and to have *you*, a fellow human, reading it. Thank you so much for being here! This book means the world to me for two reasons. The first reason is that my late dad and I often talked about publishing a range of Skinny Little Books to capture all our thoughts and ideas, with the hope of helping others navigate this crazy little thing called life. To have this dream become a reality is a special moment for me, and I'm sure he'd be super proud of achieving our goal. The second reason why this book fills me with joy, is because it was written by him.

I thought it very appropriate that the first book in The Skinny Little Book Series to be one of my dad's own creations. (And a quick spoiler alert – the next two will also be his ramblings!). I felt it right to kick things off in this way, to honour him and pave the way for what's to come. Neither of us are professional writers, we're just normal folk who used to stay up to 'the wee small hours' talking about anything and everything! Our verbal outpourings have just been captured in some kind of scribbled notes or homemade leaflets and I'm just now putting it all into a more sensible, tangible and accessible format so I can spread the cheer further!

You see, my dad was a clever old thing, and eventually, after lots of chats, exploration of ideas, and chewing the fat over a Guinness (or five!), he finally wrote down some of his own thoughts and collected wisdom from over the years.

This little book of Word Power is a compilation of inspirational quotes and statements that he gathered along the way through his various experiences of life, and he actually created homemade booklets of it to give out to people who were interested (and sometimes, who weren't!).

You may not think this particularly impressive or important, but let me set the scene.

He compiled, created and printed a booklet, back in 1998. First of all, that means every quote or statement included in this book, he either heard, read, actively researched in the library (or bookshop, which he treated like a library – maybe I'll tell you that story another time!), or thought of himself. He was not glued to a smart phone with access to quick search engines on the World Wide Web! You'll also see in his introduction that he states his efforts in trying to locate the original author for the quotes, which means he painstakingly tried to research each one; again without speedy Wi-Fi giving him instant answers. And for this reason, maybe more than any other, I believe that the quotes and statements he included were ones that meant the most to him, because he remembered them. Each quote not only had a meaning for him, but he included it with the intention of benefiting others. There was great thought and emotion behind it. Another example of human experience.

Of course, when preparing this for publication, I had the option of very quickly locating original authors and ensuring the correct wording of quotes, as the world is literally at my fingertips nowadays, but I chose not to. I wanted to publish his booklet, the way he compiled it, in its raw and original form, including any spelling or grammar mistakes, and any duplication of quotes (it wouldn't surprise me if he did this on purpose, just to make sure you were paying attention). Altering it would have lost some of that inspirational quality that he created. So, I'll reiterate what he says, neither him or myself take any credit for the quotes within, and we're aware not all have been credited. If you're interested in linking an author to a particular quote, then I'm certain a quick search on the internet will do the trick. You will also notice that he hasn't put his name to the statements that he penned. His intention was never for glory or praise, but instead, to spread inspiration and motivation for others to help themselves improve their own journey through life. I know I'm biased, but I think that's an admiral quality to have.

Secondly, creating a homemade booklet in 1998 also meant he had to type up his handwritten notes onto an old computer (which was the size of a washing machine back then!), to then scratch his head figuring out which way round the paper went to print it out double sided, allowing it to be folded into a booklet. The time, energy and dedication it took to produce these booklets is not to be overlooked. It may have been time consuming, but it was a labour of love.

As I typed up his creation, I could literally hear his voice coming off the page. I know many who knew him will also feel this when they read his introduction, and giggle at some of the more light-hearted quotes he included, and I hope others who didn't know him will get a sense of his infectious character. It's in these moments that we recognize not only the significant impact that loved ones have upon us, but also the ripple effect they can have on others. I endeavour to do just that with my own future publications.

So, I humbly ask you to please help me fulfil our intention of helping others, by sharing this little book with friends, family and strangers. It might make a nice gift for those close to you, or perhaps you might leave a copy on your seat as you leave the restaurant, for the next beautiful human to experience. I'll leave it up to you to decide.

You may have heard most, if not all, of the included quotes, but I want you to slow down and re-connect with each one, as we often skim over the meaning or miss the deeper message. There is nearly a quote for every day of the year, so I suggest you read through the book cover to cover, then get into the habit of opening it up each day to a random page and read whatever quote you are intuitively drawn to. Take some time to think deeply about the message you can take from each one in relation to your current life situation. Over time, I'm sure you'll develop favourites, just as I have.

I'm delighted to know that by bringing his scribblings up to date in these modern times, will leave a lasting imprint through this physical book. I'm pretty sure dad will be smiling from ear to ear, realizing not only are we creating the positive ripple effect we always talked about, but also because maybe one day libraries and bookshops will be a thing of the past, but somebody, *you*, will still be able to hold this book and flick through the pages for connection, inspiration, study, hope and growth.

Thank you once again for being here. I hope you understand now that this is more than just another skinny little book on the shelf. It holds meaning and memory for myself and my family, and it will in time, also mean something to you as you journey through the words and create your own experience, blending the content of this book with your own thoughts and reality. In true fashion, it's Number 148 in a nutshell.

So, with all that being said, it's my pleasure to pass you over now to my dad……

1 INTRODUCTION

"Words form the thread on which we string our experiences."
Aldous Huxley

Words are wonderful things. They can do lots of things. Have you noticed?

Words educate. Words warn. Words scare. Words motivate and inspire. They encourage and yet they can demoralise. Words can lift us to the highest heights one moment, and a moment later an arrangement of different words can dash us to the deepest of depths.

The following smorgasboard of words is intended to be of the uplifting variety. Some will educate. Some will inspire. Some will encourage. And some may just amuse. They have been collected over a long time during my own reading and research as a consultant and trainer.

Unfortunately, it is not always possible (well, it wasn't' for me) to confirm the original oysters of all these pearls. Some sayings have been passed down a long relay of messengers and the ancestral lineage has become somewhat blurred, if not entirely obliterated.

And sometimes I have noticed that a quotation has been credited to more than one person. And since many of these orators have passed on, I have no desire to contact them for clarification. I have given sources where I could.

And just for sheer devilment I have even thrown a smattering of my own originals into the pot and haven't even put my name to them. So there!

There is no real definite order or logical arrangement of the sayings which follow. I thought that if I arranged them neatly under headings and topics, you may fall into the trap of all those who slavishly obey logic, and track down only that which you were interested in at the time. By doing so you would fail to unearth the value in all those things in which you have no interest.

From time to time you may notice a few sayings relating to a common topic have been grouped together. But you may just discover other ones in isolation somewhere else in the book.

In the world we have planters, harvesters, distributors and consumers. And in this world of today they are usually different people and seldom, if ever, do they meet each other. In compiling this collection, I have had the fortunate opportunity of donning the mantle of all four.

You may not agree with all these sayings. Sometimes consumers do not have a taste for the products which distributors offer them from the harvest of the planter.

But why not just nibble your way through the delicacies on the platter. And I suggest that you revisit the table now and again. Who knows, you may find an appetite you didn't know you had.

So eat up, and feel free to lift anything off the plate which titillates your palate. Bon appetite.

2 WORD POWER

Words To Get You Going And Keep You Going

1. An open mind is not the same as an empty mind.

2. Narrow minds live narrow lives.

3. When you're the lead dog in the park, the scenery's better.

4. Live life on purpose and live life with purpose.

5. Everything matters.

6. Old familiar problems are more comfortable than strange new one.

7. Goals are marker posts you drive into your future landscape between where you are and where you want to be.

8. Excellence is not an act, but a habit.

9. Old age is like everything else. To make a success of it you've got to start young. *Fred Astaire*

10. Don't run with the easy crowd.

11. Don't wait for your ship to come in - swim out to it.

12. I might be daft, but I'm not stupid.

13. Attitudes are contagious. Is yours worth catching?

14. A true friend is someone who is there for you when he'd rather be anywhere else.

15. Money doesn't always bring happiness. People with nine million pounds are no happier than people with eight million pounds.

16. The worst thing about a bore is not that he won't stop talking but that he won't let you stop listening.

17. Experience is the one thing you have plenty of when you're too old to get the job.

18. A great deal of what we see depends on what we are looking for.

19. Vision is seeing the cathedral as we mix the

mortar.

20. The two hardest things to handle in life are failure and success.

21. Failing is not about falling down – failing is about staying down.

22. Lurking behind every adversity is a lesson and an opportunity.

23. Whatever doesn't kill me makes me stronger. *Nietzsche*

24. You can regard the rose bush as having thorns, or the thorn bush as having roses. It's entirely up to you.

25. You can't problem solve with the same knowledge that created the problem.

26. If you always do what you've always done, you'll always get what you've always got.

27. There aren't too many people on their death bed who wish they had spent more time at the office.

28. Diplomacy is thinking twice before saying nothing.

29. Measure twice and cut once.

30. Life is like a good book. The further you get into

it, the more interesting it becomes.

31. Hospitality is making your guests feel at home even though you wish they were.

32. You are a product of your environment, so choose it well.

33. No man is an island.

34. Keep away from people who try to belittle your ambitions. Small people always do that, but the really great make you feel that you too can become great. *Mark Twain*

35. You can't be all things to all people.

36. I don't know the key to success, but the key to failure is trying to please everybody. *Bill Cosby*

37. Respect cannot be purchased, leased or acquired – it can only be earned.

38. A man who always keeps both feet firmly on the ground will never get his trousers on.

39. If you want the rainbow you've got to put up with the rain.

40. You have to break eggs to make an omelette.

41. Success is more attitude than aptitude.

42. It ain't what you do – it's the way that you do it.

43. Whether you think you can or think you can't – you're right.

44. Belief is the most powerful drug in the world.

45. Our lives are moulded by our expectations – so expect the best.

46. Whatever you do, don't take yourself too seriously.

47. I don't want to achieve immortality through my work; I want to achieve it through not dying. *Woody Allen*

48. After you've heard two eye-witness accounts of the same accident it makes you wonder about history.

49. History is a con trick we play on the dead.

50. If opportunity doesn't knock, build a door. *Milton Berle*

51. Nothing lasts forever – not even your troubles.

52. It's a long road that has no turnings.

53. Today is the first day of the rest of your life.

54. Stay alive, stay awake and stay alert.

55. Learning to learn is the most fundamental learning of all. *Peter Honey*

56. Experience is not what happens to you but what you make of what happens to you. *Aldous Huxley*

57. The real voyage of discovery consists not in seeking new landscapes but in having new eyes. *Proust*

58. Forever approach life with fresh eyes and fresh ears and you will never be bored.

59. 20% of what you do produces 80% of the results, and 80% of what you do produces only 20% of the results. A wonderful lesson for those who are charged with allocating resources.

60. Efficiency is about doing things right. Effectiveness is about doing the right things right.

61. If I don't know I don't know, I think I know. If I don't know I know, I think I don't know. *R. D. Laing*

62. In every work of genius we recognise our own rejected thoughts, they come back to us with a certain alienated majesty. *Ralph Waldo Emerson*

63. A meeting is where we keep minutes and lose hours.

64. Too bad that all the people who know how to run the country are busy driving taxi cabs and cutting hair. *George Burns*

65. Irony is when you buy a suit with two pairs of trousers and then burn a hole in the coat.

66. "Lord please grant me patience. And do it NOW!"

67. Champions keep playing until they get it right. *Billie Jean King*

68. If you refuse to accept anything but the best you very often get it.

69. You become successful by helping other people become successful.

70. You get what you want by helping enough people to get what they want.

71. Talk to people about themselves and they will listen to you for hours. *Benjamin Disraeli*

72. What the mind of man can conceive and believe it can achieve.

73. No-one can make you feel inferior without your

consent. *Eleanor Roosevelt*

74. A man convinced against his will is of the same opinion still.

75. The only way to get the best of an argument is to avoid it. *Dale Carnegie*

76. All limitations are self-imposed.

77. If you can't say something good about someone don't say anything at all.

78. Criticisms are like homing pigeons. They will eventually come home to roost.

79. If you keep telling someone how great they are, they will eventually believe it.

80. People are the first creatures of emotion and then creatures of logic.

81. Great people show their greatness by the way they treat little people.

82. Treat every person you meet as if they are the most important person in the world.

83. Be wiser than other people if you can; but do not tell them so. *Lord Chesterfield*

84. Co-operation is always more productive than

competition.

85. Use what talents you possess. The woods would be very silent if the only birds that sang were those that sang best.

86. Winners never quit and quitters never win.

87. Those who preserve their character remain unshaken by the storms of daily life. They do not stir like leaves on a tree or follow the herd where it runs. In their mind remains the ideal attitude and conduct of living. This is not something given to them by others. It is their roots. It is strength that exists deep within them. *Anonymous Native American*

88. If you fail to plan, you plan to fail.

89. If you're not fired with enthusiasm, you just might be.

90. Make sure that those who say it can't be done are not standing in the way of those who are already doing it.

91. If someone doesn't give you a smile, leave one of yours.

92. A good way to make someone feel good is to remember their name, and use it.

93. Exclusive attention to the person who is speaking to you is very important.

94. People prefer good listeners to good talkers.

95. God gave us two ears and one mouth. It is often wise to use them in that proportion.

96. It is often beneficial to enquire how other brains view the topic of our own interest.

97. First, try to understand; and then to be understood.

98. Success in dealing with people depends on a sympathetic grasp of the other person's viewpoint.

99. Find a job you love and you'll never have to work.

100. You die if you worry, you die if you don't – so why worry.

101. It's pointless worrying over something you cannot influence.

102. The biggest part of success is showing up.

103. My interest is in the future because I'm going to spend the rest of my life there. *Charles F. Kettering*

104. Your future is not what it used to be.

105. My past may be a bit dodgy but my future is spotless.

106. All processes will drift to get worse if left alone.

107. When strong winds blow, some people build walls – others build windmills.

108. Nostalgia is a thing of the past.

109. Improvement is simply about making your best better.

110. If you only look at what is you might never attain what could be.

111. Be careful not to take short-term decisions with long-term regrets.

112. Soak in the 'now'. And squeeze out the bits you need later.

113. Life is where you are.

114. Life is progressing with accelerating acceleration.

115. When anything is going wrong, ask "How would I feel if this was all right?'

116. If you're not enjoying yourself, you're wasting your time.

117. When you start out to climb a ladder, make sure it's against the right wall.

118. Teamwork is the ability to work together towards a common vision.

119. Snowflakes are one of nature's most fragile things, but just look at what they can do when they stick together.

120. Necessity is the mother of invention.

121. The best way to learn something is to teach it.

122. A man can succeed at almost anything for which he has unlimited enthusiasm. *Charles M. Schwab*

123. The mind is like a parachute. It works best when it's open.

124. You're only once round the garden so smell the roses while you're there.

125. A banker is someone who lends you his umbrella when the sun is shining and wants it back the minute it rain. *Mark Twain*

126. Remember that the volume knob also turns to the left.

127. One good thing about being young is that you are not experienced enough to know that you cannot

possibly do the things you are doing. *Gene Brown*

128. Always be aware of how what you do is helping others.

129. Do unto others as you would have others do unto you.

130. Rob a child of self esteem and you will scar him for life.

131. Every process can do two things – add cost or add value.

132. You only have power over people so long as you don't take everything away from them. But when you've robbed a man of everything he's no longer in your power – he's free again. *Aleksandr Solzhenitsyn in 'The First Circle'*

133. Don't try to negotiate with someone who has nothing to lose.

134. Values fuel the engine of life.

135. You can lead a horse to water but you can't make him drink.

136. Knowing your problem is the first step towards finding a solution.

137. Who cares more about the prize rosette? The

animal or the owner?

138. A stitch in time saves nine.

139. If you want to know how good a leader you are, turn around see who's behind you.

140. Trust, train and inform your people and they will reward you many times.

141. Everyone has the capacity to think. Nowhere is it written in stone that managers do it best.

142. Surround yourself with people who are cleverer than you.

143. Let the people who do the work do the work.

144. Being left alone can be a major plus.

145. Think about a time when you did a particularly good job. Then think where your boss was at the time.

146. When you think about how much money you have made for your boss, does it give you any ideas at all?

147. Only you can think for you.

148. It's not what an author puts into a book which is important, but what the reader takes out of it.

149. An expert is someone who knows more and more about less and less.

150. If it is to be it's up to me.

151. If you are not impressed by you, how can you expect others to be?

152. Sales are more dependent on the attitude of the salesperson than the attitude of the customer.

153. If you don't know where you want to get to, any road will do.

154. ….. lead from a place in time that assumes you are already there, and that is determined even though it has not happened yet. *Stanley M. Davis, Future Perfect*

155. It is not the acquisition of knowledge which is important, it is the application. *Dr Edwards Deming*

156. He who does not use knowledge has no advantage over he who does not have the knowledge.

157. What we have to do we learn by doing.

158. Only knowledge that is used sticks in your mind.

159. We don't pay people for what they know. We pay them for what they do with what they know.

160. A learning, growing mind is an open mind.

161. People support best that which they help create.

162. The lack of money is the root of all evil. *George Bernard Shaw*

163. Goals are for the future. Values are for now.

164. Try being a boss without being bossy.

165. There is no such thing as failure.

166. When you go for something don't come back until you get it. *W. Clement Stone*

167. Whenever you get a lemon, always think about how you can turn it into lemonade.

168. I am not discouraged, because every wrong attempt discarded is another step forward. *Thomas Edison*

169. Even eagles sometimes need a push.

170. If you knew you could not possibly fail, what would you do for the rest of your life?

171. You will never succeed while smarting under the drudgery of your occupation, if you are constantly haunt with the idea that you could succeed better

in something else. *Orison Swett Marden*

172. You should not be worrying about 'how to', if you're attempting something that no-one has ever done before.

173. I do not believe in a fate which falls on men, however they act: but I do believe in a fate that falls on them unless they act. *G. K. Chesterton*

174. You can drop your own personal history whenever you want.

175. The most useful things to learn are the things you learn after you know it all. *Harry S. Truman*

176. With your thoughts you create your world. So choose your thoughts with care.

177. For every person who dreams of making fifty thousand pounds, a hundred people dream of being left fifty thousand pounds. *A. A. Milne*

178. Rehearse the future as it is desired. *William Moulton Marston, Psychologist*

179. If only youth knew; if only age could.

180. A wise man will make more opportunities than he finds. *Francis Bacon*

181. Headstones are for the living; they're no good to

the dead.

182. Money, deceit or intelligence. Three ways to settle any debt. *Chinese proverb*

183. When you know what you want, and when you know why you want it, the 'how' reveals itself.

184. When the student is ready the teacher will appear.

185. To get a tag on your values, ask yourself – "How would I like to be remembered?".

186. At eighteen our convictions are hills from which we look; at forty five they are caves in which we hide. *F. Scott Fitzgerald*

187. People quickly fulfil the expectations we have of them.

188. We are what we think. All that we are arises with our thoughts. With our thoughts, we make our world. *The Buddha*

189. The best way to predict the future is to create it.

190. Do not follow where the path might lead; go instead where there is no path and leave a trail.

191. Your attitude determines your altitude.

192. The words with which you communicate

determine the quality of your life.

193. You have to think anyway, so why not think big. *Donald Trump*

194. To become rich, think rich.

195. If things go on the way they are there'll be no change.

196. There is one quality which one must possess to win, and that is definiteness of purpose, the knowledge of what one wants, and the burning desire to possess it. *Napoleon Hill*

197. Our deepest fear is not that we are inadequate. Our deepest fear is that we are powerful beyond measure. It is our light, not our darkness, which frightens us most. *Marianne Williamson*

198. The human mind cannot hold simultaneously two conflicting thoughts. So it's up to you whether it's a positive or negative.

199. A mind once stretched by a new idea never regains its original dimensions.

200. I think, therefore I am. *Descartes*

201. You already are what you want.

202. Science rewards the creative imagination.

203. Imagination is more important than knowledge. *Albert Einstein*

204. Start with the end in mind.

205. Questions are more important than answers. Once an answer is given it immediately becomes redundant.

206. If you want to help someone learn, offer them good questions rather than good advice.

207. Failure cannot live with persistence.

208. Science understands that discoveries come by vision fed by intuition and apparent accidents. *Kathleen Stein, Omni*

209. The best way to develop the best in a person is through appreciation and encouragement.

210. Appreciation comes through the heart, flattery comes through the teeth.

211. Most people you will ever meet are hungering for understanding. Give it to them and they will love you.

212. Conversation should have three parts – a beginning, a middle and an end. Use praise and be positive in the beginning and end parts. And be careful how you handle the middle bit.

213. Bait the hook to suit the fish.

214. What counts is what works.

215. We often get deprived of a better future by the seemingly harmless tenacity of our old solutions.

216. People are interested in themselves morning, noon and night When you get your group photograph, who is the first person you look for?

217. If you don't like someone, don't be surprised if they don't like you back.

218. We are interested in others when they are interested in us.

219. Action speaks louder than words.

220. We are judged by our actions, not our proclamations.

221. If a person offends you and you are in doubt as to whether it was intentional or not, do not resort to extreme measures; simply watch your chance and hit him with a brick. *Mark Twain*

222. There is no better therapy for the pain accompanying rejection than to throw yourself right back into your work.

223. Any business you're involved with resolves around human beings.

224. People rarely succeed at anything unless they have fun doing it.

225. You can be as happy as you make your mind up to be.

226. A man without a smiling face must not open a shop. *Chinese proverb*

227. Put colour and a bit of pizzazz into everything you do.

228. You put your signature on everything you do, even if you can't write.

229. Your reputation is more precious than gold.

230. No matter what you face in life, if your passion is great enough you will find the strength to succeed.

231. The key to happiness is having dreams. The key to success is making those dreams come true.

232. Think about something you would do, even though you weren't getting paid for it; and you're well on your way to unearthing your mission in life.

233. One man cannot do right in one department of

life whilst he is occupied in doing wrong in any other department. *Ghandi*

234. Everyone lives by selling something. *Robert Louis Stevenson*

235. Everything starts with a good idea.

236. A weed is a plant whose virtues have not been discovered. *Emerson*

237. A rose may smell better than a cabbage, but it doesn't make as good a soup.

238. Great oaks from tiny acorns grow.

239. Seek and you shall find.

240. Ask and you shall receive.

241. The way to avoid mistakes is to gain experience. They way to gain experience is to make mistakes.

242. Attitudes are contagious. Is your worth catching?

243. Experts don't always know best.

244. Definition of an 'expert' – An 'ex' is a has been; and a spurt is a drip under pressure.

245. When you are confronted by 'important' and

'powerful' people, just picture them using toilet paper.

246. The most important skill you have in life is your ability to communicate.

247. Leadership falls to the person who can talk well.

248. To develop self-confidence, feel the fear and do it anyway; and get a record of successful experiences behind you.

249. If you have the flame of knowledge, let others light their candle off it.

250. We make a living by what we get. We make a life by what we give.

251. You have more control over what you give than what you get.

252. Think what would happen if each side in a partnership agreed to give 90% and accept 10%.

253. Everything you say and do is a reflection of the inner you.

254. You can't get people to believe in you until you believe in yourself.

255. Change your 'buts' into 'ands' and just see what happens.

256. Praise and encouragement are sunshine to the delicate flower of the human spirit.

257. Abilities and ambitions wither under criticism; they blossom and grow under encouragement.

258. We were not born with the skill of judgement. That comes some time later in life.

259. When opportunity knocks, the entrepreneur is always home.

260. When one door closes another opens.

261. Everything comes to him who hustles while he waits. *Thomas E. Edison*

262. It's not what you know, but who you know.

263. I have never let my schooling interfere with my education. *Mark Twain*

264. Colleges can produce graduates but they can't produce competence.

265. Avoid hangovers – stay drunk.

266. When a man's education is finished, he is finished.

267. In the land of the blind, the one-eyed man in king.

268. Wealth and fame are like salt water; the more we drink the thirstier we become.

269. It's cheaper to drag the Joneses down to your level.

270. You become successful the moment you start moving towards a worthwhile goal.

271. This too shall pass.

272. Treat the earth well. Consider it not as a gift from our parents, but on loan from our children.

273. Money only has value when it is exchanged for something useful.

274. We don't do things or buy things just for the things. We do it for the feeling it gives us.

275. A hundred years from now it will not matter what my bank account was, the sort of home I lived in or the kind of car I drove; but the world may be different because I was important in the life of a child.

276. Children are always the only future the human race has; teach them well.

277. To become the kind of person you want to be, act like the kind of person you want to become.

278. Your life is defined by your beliefs and your convictions of who you are.

279. Evil triumphs when good men do nothing.

280. Work on yourself more than you do on your job.

281. Our doubts are traitors and make us lose the good we might win by fearing to attempt.

282. The greatest ignorance is to reject something you know nothing about.

283. If you are not contributing to the solution of a problem, you are part of the problem yourself.

284. Doctors are men who prescribe medicines of which know little, to cure diseases of which they know less, in human beings of whom they know nothing. *Voltaire*

285. Always be wary that facts do not get in the way of the truth.

286. Today's news is tomorrow's fish and chip wrapper.

287. Policemen are numbered in case they get lost. *Spike Milligan*

288. An optimist is someone who does a crossword puzzle in ink.

289. Even God cannot change the past.

290. The pessimist sees the glass half empty; the optimist sees it half full.

291. There are no pockets in a shroud.

292. One of the best ways to gain experience is through experience.

293. If you are healthy you don't need exercise; if you are sick you shouldn't take it.

294. I can resist everything except temptation.

295. If it weren't for the patients, a hospital would be a brilliant place to work.

296. All work and no play makes Jack a dull boy. All play and no work makes Jack unemployable.

297. If you really want to see the incredible potential you have – step outside your comfort zone.

298. Unless you try to do something beyond what you have already mastered you will never grow.

299. The longest journey begins with a single step.

300. Be the architect of your own future. Take the personal responsibility.

301. We've been taught to look outside ourselves for sustenance – to look beyond the self.... for fulfilment... but it's possible to reverse our gaze from outward to inward. And when we do, we find an energy we've not previously identified. *Dr Wayne Dyer*

302. In everything in life, we do things not because we have to, but because we choose to.

303. It is not what happens to you that matters. It is how you choose to respond to what happens to you.

304. Never tramp on anyone on your way up in case you meet them on your way down.

305. Your life is the product of your thinking.

306. Live your dreams, you deserve it.

307. All you need to succeed is a dream, and the courage to grab it with both hands.

308. ...... the only thing we have to fear is fear itself. *Franklin D Roosevelt*

309. The big print giveth, the small print taketh away.

310. Procrastination is the thief of time.

311. Carpe Diem – seize the day.

312. Money is like manure. Just piling it up does no good; you need to spread it about.

313. Sometimes we don't need new advice; there's often enough old stuff left over.

314. Examinations are formidable even to the best prepared, for the greatest fool may ask more than the wisest man can answer.

315. A man who has never gone to school may steal from a freight car, but if he has a university education he may steal the whole railroad. *Franklin D. Roosevelt*

316. The past does not equal the future.

317. What we don't know would make a great book.

318. If I had a lower IQ I could enjoy a conversation with you.

319. You cannot unthink what you have just thought.

320. Learning is a treasure which accompanies its owner everywhere.

321. Concerning all acts of initiative and creation, there is one elementary truth – that the moment one definitely commits oneself, the Providence moves

too. *Goethe*

322. We will either find a way or make one. *Hannibal*

323. Life is either a daring adventure or nothing. *Helen Keller*

324. The secret of life is learning how to use pain and pleasure instead of having pain and pleasure use you. If you do that, you're in control of your life. If you don't, life controls you. *Anthony Robbins*

325. If you are distressed by anything external, the pain is not due to the thing itself but your own estimate of it; and this you have the power to revoke at any moment. *Marcus Aurelius*

326. The beginning of a habit is like an invisible thread, but every time we repeat the act we strengthen the strand, add to it another filament, until it becomes a great cable and binds us irrevocably, thought and act. *Orison Swett Marden*

327. Give me a lever long enough and a prop strong enough. I can single-handedly move the world. *Archimedes*

328. Some men dream of things as they are and say "Why?" I dream of things that never were and say "Why not?". *George Bernard Shaw*

329. Nothing happens unless first a dream. *Carl Sandburg*

330. Tomorrow's Utopia is merely today's flesh and blood.

331. We first make our habits and then our habits make us. *John Dryden*

332. Take away the cause and the effect ceases. *Miguel de Cervantes*

333. Action and consequence are two ends of the same stick. *Stephen Covey*

334. We are what we repeatedly do. *Aristotle*

335. We lift ourselves by our thought; we climb upon our vision of ourselves. *Orison Swett Marden*

336. It is only with the heart that one can see rightly; what is essential is invisible to the eye. *Antoine de Saint – Exupery.*

337. If we all did what we are capable of doing, we would literally astound ourselves. *Thomas A. Edison*

338. We are not limited by our old age; we are liberated by it. *Stu Mittleman*

339. The great man is he who does not lose his child's heart. *Mencius*

340. Precious are all things that come from friends.

341. Whatever you can do, or dream you can do, begin it. Boldness has Genius, Power and Magic in it. *Goethe*

342. Go for it.

343. Do it now.

344. You'll always miss 100% of the shots you don't take.

345. Out of your actions flow the rest of your life.

346. Every day, in every way, I am getting better and better.

347. The worst picture you could ever imagine is to be sitting in your rocking chair with your time running out and a basket-full of "if onlys" at your feet.

ABOUT THE AUTHOR

Hi, it's me again.
Apparently, this section is to share a little bit about me, so here goes!

I'm Nikki McMillen and I'm a Therapeutical Health Coach, based in Northern Ireland, who specialises in reducing chronic stress to help people improve their health and boost their happiness. I do this by combining new scientific methods with lessons I've learnt from my own personal journey out of stress and chronic illness.

I've been involved in the Health, Fitness and Leisure industry my whole life, with roles ranging from competitive National Sports, Gym Manager, Community Health & Well-Being Officer, founding a female-only Fitness Franchise, and acceptance onto an advisory board for NICE guidelines.

I'm super-duper passionate about strengthening communities, and helping individuals confidently take ownership and control of their own physical, mental, emotional and spiritual health, to become more resilient to life's challenges, avoid burnout, and fulfil their potential.

I'm excited for the future, as our society embarks on a more compassionate and mindful existence, and I'm grateful that I can contribute to the personal and community-wide growth of movement, mindset, health and happiness.

See ya in the next Skinny Little Book!
(waves frantically)

Printed in Great Britain
by Amazon